Animal Attack and Defense

CLEVER CAMOUFLAGE

Kimberley Jane Pryor

Marshall Cavendish
Benchmark

New York

This edition first published in 2010 in the United States of America by
MARSHALL CAVENDISH BENCHMARK.

MARSHALL CAVENDISH BENCHMARK
99 White Plains Road
Tarrytown, NY 10591
www.marshallcavendish.us

First published in 2008 by
MACMILLAN EDUCATION AUSTRALIA PTY LTD
15–19 Claremont Street, South Yarra 3141

Visit our website at www.macmillan.com.au or go directly to www.macmillanlibrary.com.au

Associated companies and representatives throughout the world.

Library of Congress Cataloging-in-Publication Data

Pryor, Kimberley Jane.
   Clever camouflage / by Kimberley Jane Pryor.
      p. cm. – (Animal attack and defense)
   Includes index.
   Summary: "Discusses how animals use camouflage to protect themselves from predators or to catch prey"–
Provided by publisher.
   ISBN 978-0-7614-4420-6
   1. Camouflage (Biology)–Juvenile literature. I. Title.
   QL759.P79 2009
591.47'2–dc22

                                                                          2009004997

Edited by Julia Carlomagno
Text and cover design by Ben Galpin
Page layout by Domenic Lauricella
Photo research by Claire Armstrong and Legend Images

Printed in the United States

Acknowledgments
The author and the publisher are grateful to the following for permission to reproduce copyright material:

Cover and title page photo of zebras © Getty Images/James Hager

Photos courtesy of: © Robert E. Barber/Alamy/Photolibrary, 22; © Visual & Written SL/Alamy/Photolibrary,
26; © Otto Rogge/ANTPhoto.com, 19; © Densey Clyne/Auscape, 25; © Amy Gulick/Auscape, 24; © Serban
Enache/Dreamstime.com, 30 (left); © Jxpfeer/Dreamstime.com, 21; © Getty Images/Altrendo Nature, 18; ©
Getty Images/Anthony Bannister, 28; © Getty Images/Fred Bavendam, 20; © Getty Images/DEA/C. DANI, 13;
© Getty Images/Georgette Douwma, 15; © Getty Images/Gerry Ellis, 4; © Getty Images/Michael & Patricia
Fogden, 11; © Getty Images/Jeff Foott, 14; © Getty Images/James Hager, 12; © Getty Images/ Tim Laman, 5;
© Getty Images/Purestock, 16; © Getty Images/Riccardo Savi, 27; © Getty Images/Mike Severns, 29; © Getty
Images/Gail Shumway, 8; © Timothy Kingston/iStockphoto.com, 6; © Goh Siang/iStockphoto.com, 9; © Roger
Whiteway/iStockphoto.com, 17; Photolibrary/Fred Bavendam, 30 (right); Photolibrary/Juniors Bildarchiv, 7;
Photolibrary/Harold W Hoffman, 10; Photolibrary/Coleman Ray, 23.

While every care has been taken to trace and acknowledge copyright, the publisher tenders their apologies
for any accidental infringement where copyright has proved untraceable. Where the attempt has been
unsuccessful, the publisher welcomes information that would redress the situation.

For Nick, Ashley, and Thomas

1 3 5 6 4 2

Contents

Glossary Word

When a word is printed in **bold**, you can look up its meaning in the glossary on page 31.

Clever Camouflage.......

Types of Camouflage

Animals use many different types of camouflage. Some animals are the same color or pattern as their surroundings. Some animals cleverly copy the shape of something in their environment, such as a leaf. Some animals change their color to match their surroundings or their **habitats**, or even to match the season.

A leaf katydid uses camouflage to look like a leaf from a tree.

Camouflage is when colors, patterns, shapes, and **texture** help animals to blend in with their surroundings.

Predators often do not see a Malayan horned frog because it has such good camouflage.

How Camouflage Protects Animals

Camouflage helps animals to blend in with their surroundings. When camouflaged animals stay still they are very hard to see. If they are not seen, they are not caught and eaten by hungry **predators**. Camouflage also helps animals to sneak up on **prey**.

A frog's green color matches the green water plants in its natural habitat.

Vital Statistics

- **Length:** 0.4 inches to 1 foot (1 to 30 centimeters)
- **Habitat:** rain forests, forests, swamps, and deserts
- **Distribution:** every continent except Antarctica
- **Predators:** fish, toads, lizards, snakes, and birds

A Frog's Matching Color

Some frogs can change their color to a lighter or darker shade of green. They often change color if they move to a new place or if their habitat changes color.

Frogs

Many frogs are a plain green color. They match green plants perfectly.

Green frogs often perch on plants growing along the edges of ponds and swamps. Because their color matches the plants so well, they are very hard to see. Many predators do not notice them unless their call gives their position away.

Gerbils

Gerbils camouflage themselves very well. Their sand-colored fur makes them very hard to spot on desert sand.

In the desert, there are few places to hide from predators. Danger comes from all directions, even from above, where there are swooping birds. When gerbils come out of their burrows, they do not want to be seen. Their fur helps them to blend in with their sandy surroundings.

Vital Statistics

- **Length:** 3.9 to 5.9 in (10 to 15 cm)
- **Habitat:** dry, sandy deserts
- **Distribution:** Africa, Asia
- **Predators:** lizards, snakes, birds, and foxes

A Gerbil's Matching Color

A gerbil has soft pale brown or pale gray fur. These colors help it to blend in with its surroundings.

A gerbil's pale brown fur matches the color of desert sand in its natural habitat.

A Clearwing Butterfly's See-Through Wings

A clearwing butterfly's wings are either completely see-through, or see-through with black or colored edges. They shine like glass in the sunlight.

Clearwing Butterflies

Amazing clearwing butterflies are named for their transparent wings. As clearwing butterflies have see-through wings, they can "hide" while in full view of predators!

Most butterflies are brightly colored. However, clearwing butterflies have wings that are completely or mostly see-through. When clearwing butterflies rest on plants, predators see the plants through their wings, instead of seeing the butterflies.

Vital Statistics

- **Wingspan:** up to 2.4 in (6 cm)
- **Habitat:** near food plants in rain forests
- **Distribution:** Central and South America
- **Predators:** birds

A clearwing butterfly's wings are so see-through that flowers show through them.

A transparent shrimp resting on a bubble coral can only be seen up close.

Vital Statistics

- **Length:** up to 7.9 in (20 cm)
- **Habitat:** ponds, streams, and oceans
- **Distribution:** warmer parts of the world
- **Predators:** fish, turtles, and waterbirds

Shrimp

A pond or rock pool might seem to contain little or no life at first glance. However, it could be home to dozens of little glasslike shrimp. Their transparent bodies hide them from predators.

Shrimp zoom around in ponds and oceans. Some shrimp are very difficult to see, because they are almost transparent. This allows them to swim freely, without having to hide from predators. They swim forward by paddling their swimming legs, and shoot backward by flicking their fan-shaped tails.

A Shrimp's See-Through Body

Some shrimp are colorful and others are almost as transparent as water. A see-through shrimp often has brightly colored markings.

Ground birds such as nightjars are patterned like dead leaves, because they roost on the ground during the day.

Vital Statistics

- **Height:** up to 8.2 ft (2.5 meters)
- **Habitat:** most kinds
- **Distribution:** almost worldwide
- **Predators:** lizards, snakes, cats, dogs, and foxes

A Ground Bird's Pattern

Many ground birds have beautifully patterned feathers. They are decorated with spots and streaks that help them to blend in with pebbles, grasses, and leaves.

Ground Birds

Ground birds live dangerous lives, feeding and nesting within the reach of hungry predators. Patterns help them to blend in with their surroundings.

Small ground birds need to have perfect camouflage, unless they want to become tasty meals for predators. Many ground birds have patterns that help them to blend in with their surroundings. When ground birds stay still, predators overlook them. Their eggs and chicks are also patterned.

Snakes

Look no further than snakes for perfect patterns. Snakes have spots, dots, stripes, and even blotches.

On hot, steamy days, snakes shelter from predators under bushes and around piles of logs and rocks. A snake's pattern helps to disguise its shape, especially when it is coiled up or draped over branches. Snakes are often so well camouflaged that they cannot be seen until they are very close.

Vital Statistics

- **Length:** 3.9 in to 23 ft (10 cm to 7 m)
- **Habitat:** forests, woodlands, grasslands, deserts, swamps, rivers, and oceans
- **Distribution:** almost worldwide
- **Predators:** other snakes, birds, badgers, weasels, and mongooses

A Snake's Pattern

Patterns help snakes to camouflage themselves both when they are still and when they are moving. A striped snake is very hard to see when it is **slithering** through long grass.

A snake with blotched patterning can blend in with piles of dead leaves.

11

When zebras stand in a group, their black-and-white stripes make it hard to see where a single zebra begins and ends.

Vital Statistics

- **Height at shoulder:** 4.3 to 4.9 ft (1.3 to 1.5 m)
- **Habitat:** grasslands
- **Distribution:** Africa
- **Predators:** hyenas, lions, leopards, cheetahs, and hunting dogs

A Zebra's Stripes

Zebras have black-and-white stripes, and some have brown shadow stripes in between. Every zebra has a different pattern.

Zebras

Zebras are well known for their bold black-and-white stripes. The stripes help zebras blend in with long grass, which makes it difficult for predators to see them.

Zebras often live in groups. When several zebras stand together, it is difficult to see where each one begins and ends. This helps to confuse predators. They find it difficult to choose a single zebra to attack.

Clown Triggerfish

Colorful clown triggerfish are decorated with spots of different sizes. They do not even look like fish against backgrounds of corals. This makes it difficult for predators to see them.

A clown triggerfish has an incredible combination of patterns and colors. It has a brilliant yellow mouth, like a clown. It has small black spots on its back and large white spots on its belly. A clown triggerfish's eyes are well-hidden by a black band over its head.

Vital Statistics

- **Length:** 1.6 ft (50 cm)
- **Habitat:** coral reefs
- **Distribution:** Indian and Pacific oceans and the Red Sea
- **Predators:** other fish

A Clown Triggerfish's Spots

A clown triggerfish has two different groups of spots. When predators see the spots, they do not realize they are looking at a fish.

A spotted clown triggerfish blends in with corals on a coral reef.

Changing Appearance......

A flounder changes its color and pattern to match the pebbly ocean floor.

Vital Statistics

- **Length:** up to 3 ft (90 cm)
- **Habitat:** ocean floor
- **Distribution:** Pacific and Atlantic oceans
- **Predators:** other fish

A Flounder's Changing Appearance

A flounder can change its color and pattern in only eight seconds. Scientists who placed a flounder on a checkerboard saw it try to match the black-and-white squares!

Flounder

Flounder can change their color and pattern quickly so that they match a sandy ocean floor one minute, and a rocky ocean floor the next. This makes it difficult for predators to see them.

An adult flounder lies on its side on the ocean floor. It stays there, still and unseen, until it spies a fish and blasts off to catch it. When a flounder moves to a new spot, it changes its color and pattern until it matches the spot perfectly.

Cuttlefish

Seeing a cuttlefish change color is a magical experience. Spots of color chase each other across its body, like a Christmas light display. Cuttlefish can also change their shape and texture to look like rocks, sand, and seaweed.

Cuttlefish glide through the water by gently moving their skirt-like fins. When they feel threatened by a predator, cuttlefish make ripples of color flow across their bodies. Instantly they match their appearance to the color and pattern of the ocean floor.

Vital Statistics

- **Length:** 1 in to 3 ft (2.5 to 90 cm)
- **Habitat:** coastal waters
- **Distribution:** worldwide in warm seas and oceans
- **Predators:** other cuttlefish, fish, sharks, dolphins, and seals

A Cuttlefish's Changing Appearance

A cuttlefish can change color in less than one second. It can change into many colors and patterns, from bright red to sandy white.

A cuttlefish can change its color and pattern to match a sponge-covered rock.

Using Dark and Light Shading........

A shark's light belly blends with the sun-streaked water near the surface.

Vital Statistics

- **Length:** 7.9 in to 39.4 ft (20 cm to 12 m)
- **Habitat:** rivers, seas, and oceans
- **Distribution:** almost worldwide
- **Predators:** whales and other sharks

A Shark's Shading

Many sharks are dark blue or gray on top and white underneath.

Sharks

In the open ocean there are few places to hide. Sharks escape the attention of predators because they are cleverly shaded to blend in with the water.

Sharks cruise the oceans in search of prey. Their dark and light shading camouflages them from predators. Predators swimming above them see their dark backs, which blend in with the gloomy water below. Predators swimming below them look up at their light bellies, which blend in with the sunlit water near the surface.

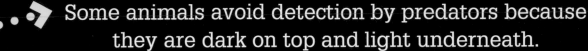
Squirrels

Squirrels dart across the forest floor, gathering seeds and nuts. Their dark and light shading helps to protect them from predators.

When the sun shines on a squirrel with dark and light shading, it lights up the back so that it matches the belly. This makes it harder for a predator to see the size and shape of the squirrel.

Vital Statistics

- **Length with tail:** 2.4 in to 3 ft (6 to 90 cm)
- **Habitat:** forests, plains, and deserts
- **Distribution:** almost worldwide
- **Predators:** snakes, birds of prey, cats, dogs, and foxes

A Squirrel's Shading

Squirrels come in many colors, including black, gray, brown, red, and white. Most squirrels have bellies that are lighter in color than their backs.

Dark and light shading helps to camouflage a squirrel's size and shape from predators.

Moths

A Moth's Shadow

The closer a moth presses itself to a surface the smaller its shadow becomes, until it almost disappears.

Moths often sit on tree trunks with their wings spread out during the day. They press themselves against the trunks so they do not make shadows. This makes it difficult for predators to see them.

Most moths are dull-colored and have **mottled** patterns. These colors and patterns help them to blend in with tree bark. When moths sit very still and flat, their camouflage becomes even better, because they do not make shadows.

When a moth flattens itself against a tree trunk, it does not make a shadow.

When the sun shines on an animal with a rounded body it makes a shadow. Some animals can flatten their bodies to make smaller shadows, so they are harder for predators to see.

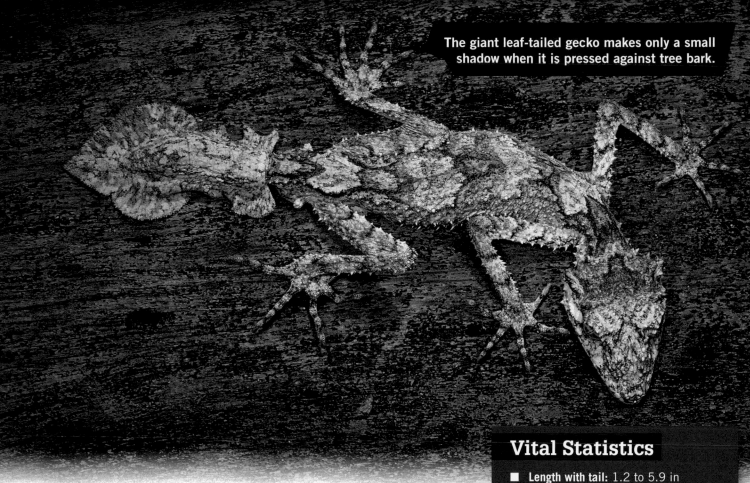

The giant leaf-tailed gecko makes only a small shadow when it is pressed against tree bark.

Geckos

Geckos are lizards with big eyes and soft skin. Some geckos have flattened bodies that make very small shadows. It is difficult for predators to see them.

Some geckos with flattened bodies do not make shadows at all. They have thin skin along the sides of their bodies and tails. This thin skin slopes down to meet the surface the gecko is resting on. This makes the gecko look flat and stops it from making a shadow when the sun comes out.

Vital Statistics

- **Length with tail:** 1.2 to 5.9 in (3 to 15 cm)
- **Habitat:** forests, deserts, grasslands, jungles, and swamps
- **Distribution:** warm parts of the world
- **Predators:** centipedes, scorpions, snakes, and birds

A Gecko's Shadow

Some geckos have flaps of skin along their tail. The flaps stop the tail from making a shadow.

Vital Statistics

- **Length:** 0.8 in (2 cm)
- **Habitat:** coral reefs
- **Distribution:** Pacific Ocean
- **Predators:** other fish

Pygmy Seahorses

Pygmy seahorses have lumps that match the color and shape of lumps on **sea fans**. This makes it difficult for predators to see them.

Tiny pygmy seahorses can blend in with two different types of sea fans. Their bodies are the same color as the stems of the sea fans. Their snouts and the lumps on their heads, bodies, and tails are the same color as the lumps on the sea fans.

A Pygmy Seahorse's Lumps and Bumps

A pygmy seahorse has lumps and bumps scattered over its body and tail. It looks like the branch of a sea fan.

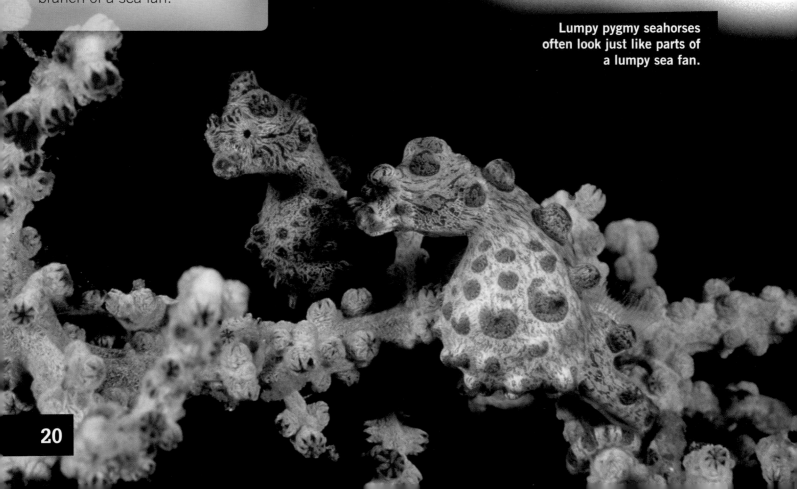

Lumpy pygmy seahorses often look just like parts of a lumpy sea fan.

A deadly reef stonefish looks like a rock on the ocean floor.

Reef Stonefish

The lumps and bumps of reef stonefish make them look like harmless rocks. However, they are the most **venomous** fish in the world.

Reef stonefish live among rocks and corals on coral reefs. They blend in perfectly with these surroundings because they are a mottled greenish-brown color. Predators and people often mistake them for rocks. People who accidentally step on reef stonefish are stabbed by their sharp, venomous spines.

Vital Statistics

- **Length:** 1.1 ft (35 cm)
- **Habitat:** coral reefs
- **Distribution:** Indian and Pacific oceans
- **Predators:** sharks and rays

A Reef Stonefish's Lumps and Bumps

A reef stonefish has lots of warty lumps and bumps. It looks like a rock covered in seaweeds, sponges, and corals.

21

Vital Statistics

- **Length:** 1.4 ft (43 cm)
- **Habitat:** seaweed-covered rocky reefs
- **Distribution:** Australia
- **Predators:** none known

A Leafy Seadragon's Copying

A leafy seadragon has leaflike parts growing from its head, body, and tail. They are used for camouflage, but not for movement.

Leafy Seadragons

Amazing leafy seadragons look just like slowly **drifting** clumps of seaweeds.

Leafy seadragons are perfectly suited to life in seaweed beds. They have large leaflike parts that look like seaweed **fronds** growing all over their bodies. Leafy seadragons also copy the green, yellow, and brown colors of seaweeds. They even copy the movement of drifting seaweeds by swimming very slowly.

A leafy seadragon copies the colors and the drifting movements of the seaweeds it lives in.

> Some animals camouflage themselves from predators by copying the appearance of something in their habitats.

An orchid mantis copies the appearance of a beautiful orchid flower.

Orchid Mantises

Exquisite orchid mantises copy the appearance of orchid flowers. Their colors match the flowers perfectly, and they have petal-like shapes on their legs.

Orchid mantises sit still on orchid flowers, waiting to eat passing insects. Their pink and white colors blend in with the flowers. The petal-like shapes on their legs make their camouflage even better. An orchid mantis can be so well camouflaged that their prey does not see it until it is too late.

Vital Statistics

- **Length:** up to 2.4 in (6 cm)
- **Habitat:** rain forests
- **Distribution:** Malaysia and Indonesia
- **Prey:** insects

An Orchid Mantis's Copying

An orchid mantis becomes more like an orchid flower as it grows up. It changes color from orange and black to pink and white.

A decorator crab dresses in seaweeds, sponges, and sea anemones to camouflage itself from predators.

Vital Statistics

- **Width:** about 1.6 in (4 cm)
- **Habitat:** rocky shores and reefs
- **Distribution:** most seas and oceans
- **Predators:** fish, turtles, and waterbirds

A Decorator Crab's "Clothes"

A decorator crab decorates itself with many objects, including seaweed, sponges, coral, and sea anemones.

Decorator Crabs

Decorator crabs look like moving gardens because they cover themselves with colorful plants and animals. These plants and animals disguise the decorator crabs from predators.

When a decorator crab spies a piece of seaweed, it snips it off with its claws. It wets the seaweed with a substance from its mouth. Then the decorator crab places the seaweed on the hooked **bristles** of its **carapace**. The substance hardens and helps the seaweed to stay in place.

A case moth caterpillar always stays in its case, which is camouflaged with leaves.

Case Moth Caterpillars

Case moth caterpillars make cases to live in that are similar to sleeping bags. They cleverly disguise the cases with twigs and leaves to protect themselves from predators.

As soon as a case moth caterpillar hatches, it makes a silk case. It decorates the case with plant materials. When a case moth caterpillar is searching for food, it drags the case along with it. When resting, it attaches the case to a tree or rock.

Vital Statistics

- **Length of bag:** 0.2 to 6 in (6 to 152 mm)
- **Habitat:** trees and shrubs
- **Distribution:** almost worldwide
- **Predators:** wasps and birds

A Case Moth Caterpillar's "Clothes"

A case moth caterpillar decorates its case with plants and other materials from its habitat. Every different type of case moth caterpillar makes another type of case.

An Arctic Hare's Winter Colors

In winter, an Arctic hare has a long, thick, soft coat of white fur. It has black fur on the tips of its ears.

Vital Statistics

- **Length:** 1.7 to 2.3 ft (53 to 69 cm)
- **Habitat:** tundra and rocky slopes
- **Distribution:** Greenland and North America
- **Predators:** owls, foxes, wolves, and weasels

Arctic Hares

No matter what the season, Arctic hares are perfectly camouflaged. This makes it difficult for predators to see them.

In summer, Arctic hares wear a bluish-gray or brownish-gray coat, which matches rocks and plants on the **tundra** around them. Before winter begins, Arctic hares replace their summer coat with a snow-white winter coat. They can hardly be seen in the sparkling snow and ice. Arctic hares that live in the far north stay white all year round, because the far north is always snowy.

An Arctic hare's white winter coat helps it to camouflage with the snow.

The white feathers of willow ptarmigans match the color of the winter snow.

Vital Statistics

- **Length:** 1.1 to 1.4 ft (35 to 44 cm)
- **Habitat:** tundra and forests
- **Distribution:** Europe, Asia, and North America
- **Predators:** hawks, owls, and foxes

Willow Ptarmigans

In winter, willow ptarmigans are pure white. They are extremely hard for predators to spot as they snuggle up in the snow to sleep.

Willow ptarmigans need to camouflage themselves because they feed and nest on the ground. In winter, both males and females become as white as the new-fallen snow. Only their tailfeathers are black.

A Willow Ptarmigan's Summer Colors

In summer, the male willow ptarmigan is red-brown on the upper part of his body, and white on the lower part. The female is red-brown with stripes and bands.

A stick insect, with its long legs and body, looks and acts exactly like a stick.

Vital Statistics

- **Length:** 1.2 to 11.8 in (30 to 300 mm)
- **Habitat:** shrubs and trees
- **Distribution:** almost worldwide
- **Predators:** spiders, lizards, and birds

A Stick Insect's Acting

A stick insect moves very slowly. It walks with a swaying motion to make itself look like a twig swaying in the breeze.

Stick Insects

Stick insects are clever actors because when they move, they look exactly like twigs swaying in a gentle breeze. This helps them to camouflage themselves from predators.

Stick insects are long and thin, like sticks. They are so well-camouflaged that they are rarely seen. Most of the time, stick insects stay perfectly still in the shrub or tree they live in. When they move, they often sway from side to side, as if blown by the wind.

Some animals not only look like an object in their surroundings, they act like the object, too.

Vital Statistics

- **Length:** up to 1 ft (30 cm)
- **Habitat:** warm seas and oceans
- **Distribution:** shallow, warm waters
- **Predators:** other fish

Frogfish

Frogfish blend in perfectly with colorful seaweed, sponges, or coral. They also act like part of their surroundings by staying very still.

Frogfish are found in many different colors, which helps them to blend in with plants and animals in their surroundings. They are often found nestled among colorful seaweed, sponges, or coral. Frogfish stay still for long periods of time, which helps them to avoid being seen by predators.

A Frogfish's Acting

A frogfish spends most of its time lying quietly near the ocean floor.

Colorful frogfish stay so still among corals that they could be mistaken for sponges.

Double Defenses

Many animals have not just one, but two ways
to defend themselves from predators.

Octopuses

Octopuses have two clever ways to defend
themselves. They use camouflage and
tricky behavior to outwit predators.

Vital Statistics

- **Length:** 0.9 in to 24.6 ft
  (2.4 cm to 7.5 m)
- **Habitat:** ocean floor
- **Distribution:** almost worldwide
- **Predators:** fish, moray eels, and sharks

An Octopus's Camouflage

Octopuses can camouflage
themselves very well. They can
quickly change their color, pattern,
and texture as they move over
different surfaces. This makes it
hard for predators to spot them.

An Octopus's Tricky Behavior

Octopuses also use tricky behavior
to escape from predators. If they are
attacked, octopuses squirt clouds of dark
ink into the water. Sometimes an octopus's
ink cloud is the same shape as the
octopus. The predator charges at the ink
cloud while the octopus zooms away.

Some octopuses can also drop one or
more arms. The crawling arms distract the
predator while the octopus sneaks away.

Glossary

Arctic	the area of land and ocean around the North Pole
bristles	stiff hairs
carapace	a hard body covering or shell
drifting	floating in a current of water
fronds	leaflike parts of seaweed
habitats	areas where animals live, feed, and breed
mottled	spotted or blotched in coloring
outline	a line showing the shape of an object
predators	animals that hunt and kill other animals for food
prey	animals that are hunted and caught for food by other animals
sea fans	corals that look like fans
slithering	sliding along the ground
texture	the roughness or smoothness of an animal
transparent	clear or easy to see through
tundra	flat areas of frozen ground with no trees
venomous	being able to make a type of poison called venom

Index